EMOTIONAL EATING

Overcome Your Eating Disorder and
Stop Overeating
Through Meditation and Intuitive
Eating, Binge No More

Contents

INTRODUCTION

Emotional eating is a component of our culture, as well. We use meals to celebrate, to cope with anger, to deal with a hard day at the job and even boredom (always sitting in front of the TV, eating unconsciously) It's component of our culture. The issue with this is that it's not seen as an issue in learning, but it's one.

We spend so much time numbing ourselves that when we don't have the opportunity to do so, we don't understand how best to cope with the feelings that occur in us. Food also has addictive physical characteristics within it that can influence our mood as well (I'll address this later in a blog article) so that everything can be overwhelming. If we don't live in the present moment and enable feelings to flow through us, but instead shake ourselves, we bring a bunch of stuff around unknowingly. Sometimes this may come up in about of aggression or some other type. The thing is, if we don't face it, don't learn to cope with our feelings, then we're just going to live a life of numbing, binging, or longing. You lose the possibilities of existence, of adopting opinions.

People suffering from this way of eating are driven to eat, so they don't have to confront what is hurting them externally. They become accustomed to the manner life is handled. That's why dieting and calorie restrictions don't function. And since most diets don't educate you about emotional eating, we're never fully conscious of it and believe it's incorrect with us

CHAPTER 1
WHAT IS EMOTIONAL EATING?

Emotional eating is when individuals use meat as a manner to cope with emotions instead of satisfying hunger. We were all there, completing a whole bag of chips out of boredom or ordering cookie after cookie while cramming for an extensive exam. But doing a lot, particularly without knowing it, can impact weight, wellness, and overall well-being.

Not many of us·are linking eating and our emotions. But knowing what causes emotional eating can assist individuals in making a difference.

One of the greatest myths about emotional eating is that it's driven by adverse emotions. Yes, individuals often switch to meals when they're stressed, solitary, sad, depressed, or tired. Emotional eating, however, can also be related to beneficial emotions, such as the romance of exchanging dessert on Valentine's Day or the celebration of a holiday.

Emotional eating is sometimes linked to significant life occurrences, such as suicide or divorce. More often than not, however, it is the many little daily stress that causes someone to find consolation or diversion in meals.

Occasionally, emotional eating is every day. Everyone's been celebrating with meals before, that's what birthday parties, Christmas lunch and BBQ's on Super Bowl Sunday and the Fourth of July are all about. But emotional eating can become a severe issue if it leads to adverse psychological and physical imbalances in our life.

Frequent emotional eating can readily turn into a damaging process. Emotional eating becomes entrenched in the lives of its sufferers when they use nutrition to regulate their mood, cope with stress, or overcome the feelings of anxiety or boredom.

This kind of behavior can readily cause mental eaters to be overweight or obese because most of them think to starve.

"Satisfying" this insatiable hunger with meat, many mental eaters eat far more calories than their body requires, and they achieve a ton of weight that becomes highly hard, if not inevitable, to lose.

There are some common signs of mental eating:

- ✓ Eating when not physically starving.
- ✓ You are eating during moments of powerful feelings, such as rage or depression.
- ✓ You are eating when you're tired.
- ✓ It's fast eating.
- ✓ You are eating right after coming back from the job.
- ✓ I am eating on its own out of confusion at the amount or sort of meat being consumed.
- ✓ I am eating until it's uncomfortable.
- ✓ Feelings of anger, depression, or guilt after overeating.

Recognizing Emotional Hunger

Recognizing Emotional Hunger (as applied to actual physical hunger) is one of the keys to overcoming or stopping frequent emotional eating.

- ✓ Some of the features of mental starvation include:
- ✓ You're not hungry for one minute, and you're hungry for the next minute.
- ✓ Emotional hunger often enthuses particular meals, such as pizza, sweets, or cheeseburger.
- ✓ Emotional hunger starts in the body and mind, not in the stomach.

- ✓ Emotional hunger often accompanies unpleasant emotions.
- ✓ Emotional hunger includes an immediate or absent-minded diet
- ✓ Passionate desire is not fulfilled when you're completed.
- ✓ Emotional hunger makes you feel guilty about it.

CHAPTER 2
WHAT ARE THE REASONS FOR EMOTIONAL EATING

People often achieve weight as a consequence of an emotional crisis in their lives. This can often be the result of a work failure, a shift in one's routine that has given comfort to their lives. However, one of the factors why individuals start to become mental eaters is the end of a partnership in which it was not entirely reciprocal. I understand this is accurate, not only because of all the studies on why individuals overeat but because I've encountered the same feelings and drives to eat in my own private lives.

Depression

Whether triggered by a chemical imbalance in the brain or a direct result of a tragic situation in one's life, it will always be detrimental to the individual's mental and therefore, physical health. This is one of the primary triggers of emotional eating. Loss of energy and involvement in products that have previously given enjoyment and happiness to the person will also lead to an increase in weight due to a rapid decrease in the rate of the practice of the person one does not see the need to get out of bed for the whole day, the absence of training will contribute to a rise in the person's weight. It's just a straightforward but sad reality, and it's the primary reason for emotional eating.

A follow-up reason why depression will contribute to a rise in one's weight is that their strength will be reduced. Their struggle to succeed will wane and, as a consequence, their willingness not to consume unsafe food will be diminished. The voice in your ear that says that it's not good to waste at McDonald's every day will be altered to state that returning to McDonald's every day is the only thing you can regulate in your lives, and that should be achieved. Besides, the individual believes about what's going to matter anyway. If one remains on this route for too long, they will readily reach the point of no exchange and discover it very hard, if not impossible, to find a way home to a healthy lifestyle

Loss of Command

The loss of power in one's destiny, which stems from an unwanted end to a partnership, is also a justification for emotional eating. Many people feel that they must be the captain of their ship and that the invisible forces that govern the lives of other peoples do not rule over them. Therefore, when something that they consider terrible happens, something that they cannot regulate, their willingness to regain control of their life, is boosted exponentially. The consumption of meat that one eats generally depends on the individual's will. A desire to restore power is a significant motive when you feel that your life has been unraveled.

These are two understandable, yet hazardous, and very unhealthful responses to the unwanted end of a partnership, and they are both things that need to be prevented from speeding up the healing process. There are many explanations for emotional eating.

If you're interested in losing weight and living a healthier lifestyle, click on my blog to figure out precisely how these objectives can come to fruition. People have been willing to do important stuff when they set their minds to the job at hand. A degree of determination, combined with the correct instruments and understanding, and anything could occur!

Believe it and begin living a healthy lifestyle that you owe to your buddies, your family, and most importantly, that's something you owe to yourself.

What Causes is Emotional Eating?

The causes of Emotional Eating are challenging to define and vary from individual to individual. However, there are some prevalent mental causes that often trigger overeating. Knowing what they are is a significant stage in the cycle of healing.

Here are some of the most common triggers of mental overeating:

1. Boredom-Boredom often contributes to restlessness and the simplest way to solve it is for most individuals to consume. The problem with eating out of boredom is that we often fail to understand how much we've consumed. It's as if our mind has lost track of what we're doing.

2. Loneliness-Often, individuals who feel solitary, particularly after a bad divorce, tend to "drop their sadness" in meals. Some food can make us feel happy if only for a short time. This isn't terrible, but it can be harmful if we want to have a long-lasting weight loss.

3. Stress—Stress is likely the most common source of binge eating. The pressure pushes our body into a kind of inner tempest of reduced trust, dread, and adverse well-being. Again, food is the principal cause of convenience to many of us. It doesn't fix any of the issues, but we're going to do it anyway.

4. Tiredness-Now that's interesting because fatigue isn't an emotion, but we often turn to food to keep us awake, especially if we have some time at work or school and can't go to bed. Food can act as a transitional reservoir of energy, but it will not heal fatigue in the lengthy run.

There are more, fewer causes for emotional eating. After you have recognized yours, the time arises to begin coping with them one by one. It could be performed.

Dealing with The Factors That Leads to Emotional Eating.

When food is consumed to fulfill one's emotions instead of fulfilling one's hunger, it results in emotional eating that has adverse implications, such as the enhanced danger of heart disease, signs of anxiety and depression, and increased risk of obesity. This research looked at the danger variables of emotional eating in the hope of providing clinicians a stronger knowledge of how to avoid or teach emotional eating. There is a multitude of threat variables for emotional eating. Emotional eating is complicated because it is affected by many variables, such as food preferences, genetics, culture, psychology, and cultural and physical climate. There are, therefore, many more danger variables than what is being explored here. However, this research tries to add emotional eating to current psychology literature. Using survey reviews, this research examined whether parental bonding was connected with emotional eating in non-clinical college learners who resided with colleagues instead of their families. Besides, this research explored whether one's level of college fitness was correlated with emotional eating. An effort to reproduce prior connections between parenting style, one transfers to college, and parental bonding was made using steps that permitted for more thorough assessment and the use of these factors as multi-regression predictors. Results suggested that perceived parental bonding and the amount of college readiness did not have a significant connection with emotional eating. However, gender and race differences in emotional eating have been recognized. Besides, gender, ethnicity, avoiding coping, and socially-supported coping estimated 27 percent of the variance seen in emotional eating suggest that treatment should focus on studying efficient coping techniques to reduce sensitive consumption. This research may also assist clinicians and dieticians to comprehend better the hazards that contribute to emotional eating.

Children with inadequate eating practices are more probable to become overweight or underweight. It seems to have become an increasingly prevalent practice today. Poor dietary habits often result from an unnecessary consumption of electricity and insufficient use of micronutrients. Although poor eating practices can only be a component of the cause, they contribute considerably to the danger of obesity and malnutrition. This can set the phase for more negative health issues (e.g., heart and liver illness), particularly if bad dietary habits are prolonged to adulthood.

Bad Habits

Over-consumption of products elevated in sugar, fat, and salt.

- ✓ You are eating unhealthful meals.
- ✓ I am eating when you're not starving.
- ✓ Refusal to consume vegetables or fruit.
- ✓ I am eating too quickly.
- ✓ To be picky eaters (to eat a restricted diet).
- ✓ Eating while watching TV, playing video / PC matches, etc. Overeating & eating convenience.
- ✓ Drinking too many sugary beverages

Skipping breakfast and dining in uneven hours.

- ✓ Chew your food at least 10 seconds before swallowing.
- ✓ Pack a home-made lunch/breakfast for college, make sure it involves a nutritious meal (e.g., sliced fruit, pure or oat sandwiches).
- ✓ Eat slowly, and it requires a few minutes for the brain to recognize that the stomach is complete.
- ✓ Drink a glass of water or a pan of soup to prevent overeating.
- ✓ Schedule time for your meal / eat on time.
- ✓ Get more fiber (e.g., whole beans and legumes).
- ✓ Eat lower servings of food.
- ✓ Drink more of the H_2O.
- ✓ Eat a range of foods per dinner.
- ✓ Choose products that are cooked, braised, or grilled instead of deep-fried.
- ✓ What parents can be an excellent role model, practice healthy eating practices, and prepare healthier products.
- ✓ Don't create a habit of dining out or ordering outside meals.
- ✓ Start promoting young people to eat healthily.
- ✓ Eat together as a family as often as possible.
- ✓ Avoid treating or promising meals as a prize.

✓ Don't force your child to eat something they don't like, gradually wean it.

✓ Play more, transfer more, be involved!

Why Do We Engage in Mindless Eating? /Reasons

Mindless eating can happen while reading, riding, learning, watching TV, socializing, or doing any activity where you concentrate on something other than eating. Before you realize it, you've consumed more than you've scheduled, or you've wasted all together unplanned. Mindless eating is generally unsatisfactory and contributes to excess weight and poor health.

Each of these calendar times is a fresh beginning, and you may feel like it's the time of year to begin clean practices. Unfortunately, however, without any follow-up, most individuals fall back into the old routine of eating unconsciously.

To obtain understanding into how often you consume unconsciously, I recommend that you take a day or a week to drink with your other side. This act requires your brain to be involved in eating. It's normal for you to consume with your other hand, so your mind must give a request to your side to pick up meat and placed it in your lap. This experiment is going to be a wake-up call for you, how often you participate in mindless eating.

Another way to stop mindless eating is to settle down every moment you consume something. Let it be awkward for you to waste while standing. After proposing this to a client to assist stop her mindless eating, I got the following email from her: "I have to inform you that when I say my child, it's time to eat, he goes to his highchair. At 16 (almost 17) months, he understands that you have to sit down to consume." Imagine your lives if you never ate thoughtlessly again. You would want to appreciate everything you choose to consume.

You can readily alter your eating style by pursuing the eight simple measures of mindful eating:

1. It's all right to be starving. Hunger is not the foe, and it is over-stuffed. Over-stuffed implies over-eating. Get comfortable feeling killing. Your body is telling you to consume. Continue eating a balanced diet with the correct quantity of meals for your body size.

2. Respect, thank and thank your flesh for any weight, even today's mass. You're going to take more exceptional care of your meat when it's valued and not belittled.

3. When you discover yourself wondering, "What should I eat," alter it to, "Why do I want to consume?" If you're thirsty, eat. By requesting another query, the

answer shifts, guiding you to a new, more efficient reaction.

4. You're neither a great nor a poor eater. Make everything you consume an intentional option, and every decision you create has either an advantage or a result of it. Be prepared to acknowledge your choice, along with the outcome.

5. Drink some water. Water is essential to your health. Often hunger is masked as thirst, and you eat when you're genuinely thirsty. Drinking water frequently every day will quench your thirst and eliminate the urge to consume unconsciously.

6. Stop creating sparks with a knife and a fork. Eat gently while you listen carefully to your breathing. When you start to sigh or breathe heavier, your stomach is full, but you don't understand it yet. It's time you stopped eating.

7. Begin to practice patience and perseverance. If you efficiently take the time to exercise the abilities you need, mindless eating will be a product of the past.

Stop over-extending yourself: Ugh. Well, you understand the routine. You have too much stuff to do, and they're all essential. So, you over-extend yourself by preparing a healthy "to - do" list all day or all week long! If this is accomplished continuously without leaving the moment to catch your breath, you are inclined to feel tired, out of command, and frustrated. These are very undesirable feelings that often contribute to emotional eating. A few methods to prevent over-extending yourself is to bring your "to - do" list and give precedence to each of your duties. Just make a contract with yourself to get the instant assignments ahead straight away and leave the remainder for another moment. Or, if all the jobs need to be accomplished straight away, consider asking relatives or colleagues to assist you. And, don't forget, while you're in the middle of checking out the items on your "to-do" list, be sure to take breaks to eat and drink to keep your energy and mood high.

Identify your requirements, please. So much emotional eating is the result of not meeting our needs. Often my clients understand that something is off, but they don't know what it is that causes pain, so they're eating. So, you need to be evident about what your demands are. I understand that sounds simple, but that's not always the case. Once you've accomplished that, find out how to meet your requirements as often as necessary, even if it includes having some unpleasant discussions with relatives or colleagues. Some negotiations may be needed, but you can get what you need so that you don't switch to meals as a means of appeasing yourself.

Be mindful of patterns and behaviors. Many of us have trends and conduct that guide us down unproductive and sometimes harmful routes in our life. One way to facilitate a healthy shift in these habits so that we don't switch to meals is to become conscious of the occurrences that often precipitate these behaviors. These take some detective work and patience, but this can be deciphered in such a way that the pattern/behavior can be changed. The best way to do this is for the next moment the undesired pattern/behavior has lifted its cap, to take some time to evaluate the day or latest occurrences that resulted to the conduct in the first location. Then see what you could do differently next time, so you're not going to experience the same outcome. This is probable to involve some tweaking along with the manner, but with patience, it is feasible to alter so that you can discover fresh patterns/comportments that create you feel empowered instead of beaten.

Stop comparing yourself with the others. We're often unhappy with our life because we're continually comparing ourselves to others. This is a useless practice, and it will never help us in any manner. When we compare ourselves to others, we're saying that whatever we have at the moment isn't lovely enough. This will always create us feel joyless, unhappy, and diminish our self-esteem and trust. A few methods to solve what I call "comparisonitis" is to remember that we are all distinctive on our routes. Instead of enabling someone else's life experiences to assess our value, we need to keep reminding ourselves that we are all on our unique journey. If all of us were to be the same, our maker would have created us that way. However, if we want a shift in our life, we can admire what others have in their life and use it to motivate us instead of enabling us to overlook what we have at the moment. Doing this will assist in eliminating "not enough" emotions that often accompany "comparisonitis."

Stop attempting to make it flawless. Stop playing the old tape in your head that one day, if you try hard enough, you're going to be perfect. Remember that perfection does not occur every day and that you are a worthy, skilled lady who, despite her apparent imperfections, affects the globe. Identify where these ideas arose (generally early infancy) and begin to break down these views to render them more realistic. Also, recount all the times in your life when you thought that something you did wasn't beautiful enough, and you were agonizing about it to find out that it was enough. Learning to tell, "It's nice enough." is going a long way to reduce perfectionist thinking.

CHAPTER 3
HOW TO EFFECTIVELY OVERCOME EMOTIONAL EATING

Overcoming Emotional

Eating Emotional eating happens when food becomes a system for dealing with emotional stress. And that implies that dieting can effectively cause more issues than it does. As an emotional eater, when you're unable to stick to a diet, the immediate emotions of guilt are soothed only by more meals, which is encountered with more guilt, more nutrition, and so on.

Here are a few suggestions to assist you in handling mental obesity take the emphasis off eating by teaching new coping skills. Find non-food methods to make yourself comfortable.

Make a list of things you can do at a moment's notice to assist in reducing your stress rate. You might be able to call your greatest buddy, snuggle with your cat, or read a section from your favorite author. Practice meditation or read the chapter of the religious text. Do a couple of yoga positions. If you think you need to bring something in your mouth, grab a glass of cold water and drink it gently. Pay attention to how great it feels in your mouth and how hydrating your whole body is.

Keep a diary. If you feel like eating something, and you're not starving, create a few notes. Why do you feel like this manner? Did something occur to you in your mental lives? Are you sad or solitary or tired? By paying attention to when those urges kick in, you may begin to realize what kind of psychological causes are causing you to indulge in. Also, be on the lookout for specific desires that correlate with particular feelings. The more you understand about the kind of meals you're looking for, and the more efficient you're going to be in seeking solutions.

Focus on maintaining your health-instead of dieting.

Instead of putting all the emphasis on calories and mentally marking' excellent' or' inadequate' products, attempt balancing your nutrition and eating healthy meals from a multitude of food groups. Exercise, eat well and get enough sleep. You might discover your feelings out when you take excellent care of yourself.

Get some assistance. If you have difficulty gaining a grip on your emotional eating, consult a counselor or psychotherapist who has expertise with emotional eating problems.

If you are willing to experience convenience without switching to food, you will be prepared to bring food in the right location in your lives. Then you can operate on integrating healthy eating practices into your day.

Why are we eating? Well, common sense informs us that we need to consume to nurture our bodies, that we need to consume to fulfill physical hunger. In reality, however, our conduct around meals is far from optimal.

It is currently projected that there are more than 1 billion overweight people worldwide, with at least 300 million of them obese. Studies have shown that 75% of US adolescents are overweight or obese (source research conducted by a group at John Hopkins University in Baltimore). Obesity rates in the United Kingdom, Canada, and Australia are quickly rising to those in the United States. Obesity is defined as a worldwide epidemic by the World Health Organization. Something has gone wrong.

People are children too much and eating the wrong kind of meals. In most instances, absence of dietary understanding is not an issue; on the contrary, overweight individuals tend to be nutritional specialists, they understand what they should be and should not eat, many have an encyclopedic knowledge of the caloric, fat and carbohydrate values of their favorite foods, yet they continue to consume the same foods, apparently with abandonment. Why? Why?

Besides eating to fulfill physical hunger, individuals also consume to satisfy mental cravings. The word "emotional eating" encompasses a whole variety of behaviors around food, including eating to fulfill and specific emotion, eating as a diversion from something, eating as a habit, eating to feel in command, eating unconsciously and for subconscious purposes.

Emotional Eating

It's natural to use meat to create you feel safer, and food has always been used in this manner in our culture. Think back to when you were a kid, were you ever given a cookie or a lollipop when you were angry? Eating our favorite meal when we feel poor is a universal approach that operates every moment. The only issue is that it only works temporarily. You only think safer while the food is in your mouth. And the kind of meals we all switch to when we feel poor tends to be high-fat, high-sugar, which is harmful to our weight loss attempts. I've never heard anyone gorge themselves on the broccoli when they feel dissatisfied!

Emotional eating is also symptomatic of deep-seated emotional baggage such as guilt, fear, solitude, and rage. This may involve treatment to clear it up. There are many presently available therapies, such as hypnotherapy and cognitive behavioral therapy, which allow an individual to discover the root of the Issue and overcome mental obstacles to weight loss.

Eating as A Diversion

People also consume as a diversion from something, for instance, using meals to procrastinate, like eating instead of getting began. the report you need to write,' I'm just going to sit down and have a cup of coffee and that donut, and then I'm going to get to work.' People also usually consume when they're weary instead of resting or sleeping, instead of having love, instead of tobacco when they give up, or because they're bored, or even because they're enthusiastic and eating makes them calm.

Eating as A Control Mechanism

People who think they have little power over their life, and this is prevalent to individuals who have poor self-esteem, may experience eating disease, because this is the one region of their life where they think they can exercise power. The irony is, of course, that eating disorders such as bulimia, anorexia, or binge can take over very quickly so that the sufferer no longer has any authority over their eating.

The majority of emotional eating is unconscious. The individual is not conscious of the subconscious purposes for eating, and they merely feel it forced to do so. Much of the subconscious conditioning that leads individuals to overeat is focused on infancy knowledge, practice, and culture, and has become part of their character.

Becoming conscious of the usual mental overeating and the causes behind those feelings is the first move on the path to conquering this harmful conduct. There are a lot of methods you can use to uncover your eating habits and cope with them.

You're more likely to give in to emotional eating if you don't have a strong support network. Lean-to family and friends or consider entering a support group.

Fight your boredom. Instead of snacking when you're not starving, distract yourself and replace for healthier conduct. Take a stroll, watch a film, play with a cat, listen to songs, read, surf the internet, or call a buddy.

Take the temptation away. Don't hold comfort food in your house hard-to-resist. And if you feel angry or blue, you're supposed to postpone it. Your trip to the grocery store until you have your emotions in check.

Don't take that away from you. If you're trying to lose weight, you may be willing to decrease calories too much, eat the same meals on an ongoing basis, and banish treatments. This can only serve to boost your food cravings, particularly in reaction to feelings. Eat adequate quantities of healthier food, appreciate occasional treatment, and have plenty of variation to assist in reducing cravings.

A good snack. If you feel the desire to consume between meals, choose a tasty snack, such as new fruit, low-fat vegetables, nuts, or unbuttered popcorn. Or attempt reduced-calorie variants of your favorite products to see if they meet your cravings.

Briefly, here are a few suggestions to assist you in solving compulsive eating.

1. Please use a food diary. When you write down everything you're consuming, and what you've been experiencing at the moment, you're going to begin seeing patterns coming up. Awareness is one of the most significant measures to overcome emotional eating.

2. Therapy-either with self-help or with a specialist. If you have unsolved feelings such as guilt, rage, fear, or poor self-esteem, consider treatment to assist you in solving these issues. Many dietitians discover healthy hypnosis and hypnotherapy for the clearing of

emotional baggage and any secondary gain problems. If you don't want to see a therapist attempt self-hypnosis that can assist you re-program your subconscious with more helpful views. CBT (Cognitive Behavioral Therapy) is also an enormously effective therapy for reconditioning eating behavior.

3. Get structured, man. Organize your workplace, a cluttered house or office can often contribute to cluttered thinking. Do you ever get the feeling that you want to be a new weight loss and exercise program, but you can't get started? This may be because the clutter is keeping you away, it's going to be evident, and it's going to begin new.

4. Set the targets. The efficacy of the goal setting is well documented, crystallizes what you are trying to accomplish and shifts from vague hope to actual intent.

5. Change your distractors, instead of eating, attempt walking or knitting! Well, whatever operates for you

1. Call A Friend

My friend began to be aware of her willingness to consume mentally, and she reached out to me for assistance. I offered her a lot of advice on this list, and the time disappeared. The next day, she woke up energized and willing to begin new.

If your friends don't occur to be wellness trainers, you can still speak to them about what you feel like. Talk about what's going on or listen to them and help them with what they're going through. Ideally, the mental eating desire would have gone at that moment.

If you don't feel safe speaking to a buddy about your emotional eating problems, it may be useful to work with a qualified specialist who will hear and provide advice particular to your condition. As a Certified Nutrition and Health Coach, I assist females in creating beneficial relationships with nutrition.

2. Waiting for the times out

Binge tends to last only a few minutes. The impulse can arrive as fast as it leaves, so sometimes you need to get over the primitive urge.

When you have a phone call with your buddy, your mood and mind may be in an entirely distinct location. You could pick up your mobile and be prepared to continue your day without inhaling a bag of chocolate.

3. Examine Your Emotions

When you're about to get a knuckle deep in a Cheetos pocket, belief about why you're going to get a snack. Is it going to fill the gap? Are you procrastinating on a challenging venture? Have you been annoyed by someone?

Eating can be a way to numb the pain or fill the gap. Think about your day and mood and see if you can target the root cause of the distress you're feeling. Then see if you can thoroughly examine the emotions you're feeling, and break it down so that it doesn't consume you and your meal decisions any longer.

Think about what you want to do. Is it company, intent, laughter? Look for other methods to meet your requirements.

4. Remember why And when

I train individuals, and I have to begin by communicating why they want to create a shift. Reasons may start by wanting to drop weight or get a new job, but when I dive more in-depth, I discover it's a lot more.

People want to have the energy to perform with their children when they're older. They're also trying to assist individuals and create a difference in the globe.

Keeping your broader objectives in mind can hold you on track when you feel volatile.

Eating a big bag of chips is not probable to assist you along the way.

5. Think about the future

If you're talking about eating another or the 10th cookie, think about how your decision will feel later today, tomorrow, next month, or next year. Are you supposed to feel excellent about that?

Then take a look at the larger image. What's the food that prevents you from doing longer—losing weight, finding the friendship you've been searching for, getting a current job?

Emotional eating and overeating often create a good deal of shame and dissatisfaction. I've experienced that much shame when I do the binge eating. I can't appreciate the meals before the guilt sets in. So, I attempt to begin with the sensation that I'm going to arrive after I make my decision to consume something. Then I choose something else to do on my list, and the time goes by.

6. Find Purpose

Whenever I go to the refrigerator, I'm just tired. I may not have planned any enjoyable social activities. Maybe I haven't reached out to a buddy in a while, so there's not much on the calendar. I can also try to prevent working on a challenging task, so I'm looking for a snack.

Staying busy can assist me with emotional eating. Whenever I work on a passion project that lights me up, it's time to fly hours before I realize I haven't eaten in hours.

Keeping your calendar full of adventures and activities that give you pleasure and intent, can assist in easing your mindless eating. If you need assistance in finding your goal, read more here.

7. Move

Movement is a significant diversion from emotional eating. I've got a couple of go-to songs that are my "battle songs." I believe everyone should have a song that picks him or her up. I like dancing to my song, but if it's not your jam, take a stroll and push your body.

Step up a few steps in the office to get your blood and adrenaline going. Do some pushups or stretches to remind yourself how powerful you are and how essential your body is. Movement can assist in easing any anxiety or stagnating feelings that are not budgeted for. Bonus points for a stroll with a buddy to get some personal time in, as well as time to speak about any urgent problems.

8. Get Outdoors

Doing your motion indoor is another beautiful thing. Not only will the light wake you up, but it will also assist you to balance your cortisol concentrations so that your energy remains strong. You want your cortisol to be up during the day and down at night when it's ##s to bed.

Whenever I get out of the woods, it enables me to see a larger image. The size and beauty of being in the forest change my mind from insignificant stuff, like salty chips, to a bigger perspective of what is essential.

9. Meditate

Whether or not you meditate (if you don't, begin here), attempt to relieve some of the stress and anxiety that you may experience by taking some deep, clean breaths. Practice lengthy, relaxed breaths to relax and get out of your head.

You can also sit in a seat with your legs under your hips and your arms comfortably in your lap. Close your eyes and swallow gently for count 4, hang on to 4 beats, and then gently exhale for another four counts. Repeat this three times and feel the distinction.

10. Sleep

I'm sure I'm not the first to inform you that it's incredibly essential to get enough sleep. Not only is it useful to your energy and brain function, but sleep can also influence your meal decisions.

If you get less than 7 or 8 hours of sleep in the evening, you might get bored and have some severe food cravings. I understand if I only get 5-6 hours, I wake up hungry and willing to consume it all, even though substantial carbs are at the bottom of the list.

11. Drink Water

Dehydration can often be what you feel like your body's hunger pangs. Whenever I feel thirsty, too, near to my last meal, I begin drinking water. After my body's moment to digest the water, I discover that my so-called hunger pangs have disappeared.

If the water feels too dull when you measure it against a stack of donuts, attempt sprucing up your beverage. Add lemon, cucumbers, ginger, mint or new fruit to your spa water that will make you feel refreshed.

12. To prevent getting too often to eat,

Take a look at the food you're presently eating. Do they have a beautiful blend of fat, fiber, and protein? Each of these parts is going to assist you fill-up. All three of you want and need to feel completely satisfied after dinner.

Healthy fat from avocados, nuts, and coconut milk will not only assist most people in functioning more effectively but will also help guarantee that you're not starving for an hour after eating. My fat lemon bombs are a significant cause of fat and a sweet treat to hit any cravings.

13. Plan Making

Your meal timetable, and when you plan to consume each of them can assist you with emotional eating. It takes the guesswork out of what you have to do and when you don't think about eating all the time.

If I'm not planning my meals, I'm starting to think about what I'm supposed to consume for dinner while I'm washing my breakfast dishes. I've been talking about it for hours, particularly when I'm attempting to prevent thinking about other urgent problems of the day. When my meals are prepared in advance, I can set my brain free for more significant operations.

Sunday is my big day of cooking. Usually, I have one (or more) of these five sauces in my fridge at all moments so that dinner or a tasty snack can come together rapidly. I'm making a lot of smoothies and protein and vegetables so all my smooth food components are prepared to go. This also enables me to prevent the temptation and the wrong meal decisions later on.

Your body works best when it comes to a periodic meal timetable so attempt and stick to one. It is going to assist both your mind and your brain.

14. Practice Self Care

When you have a miserable day, and you need to consume mentally, attempt a little self-care.

Self-care can take the form of a lot of different things. It could imply a massage, a hot shower, writing in your diary, reading an excellent book, creating a hot cup of nourishing tea, or just staying still for a little while.

It's simple to do all these things when you're in an excellent mood, but attempt and get used to doing them when you're feeling down. Let's hope that this superb mood will become more frequent.

15. Eat

If you've been through the whole list above and are still starving, then eat!

You may not have eaten enough at the last meal, or you may be recovering from a massive or cold exercise, so take care of yourself. You always want your blood sugar to be stable and your energy to be reliable.

Depriving yourself of nutrients is not supposed to create you feel any good. Just be aware of the decisions you make so that you can stop sleeping emotionally and have a good connection with your meals.

CHAPTER 4
HOW TO EMBARK ON MINDFUL AND HEALTHY EATING

Mindfulness implies concentrating on the present moment while calmly recognizing and embracing your emotions, ideas, and body sensations. "The tenets of mindfulness also extend to mindful eating, but the notion of mindful eating extends beyond the person. It also includes how what you consume impacts the universe. We consume for complete wellness," tells Dr. Cheung. That's fundamentally the same idea that led to the growth of the 2015 U.S. proposal. Dietary guidelines which, for the first moment, regarded the sustainability of food plants as well as the safety advantages of meat.

"When you consume carefully, you slow down and recognize your feelings and hunger so that you can drink when you're exhausted and taste the meat in your mouth, "says Jennifer Taitz, Psy. D., an LA-based psychologist and author of End Emotional Eating and How to Be Single and Happy. Two of the most significant advantages of conscious eating is that it decreases a ton of stress around eating (after all, you're only eating when you need to!) and can assist individuals to appreciate their meals more, she claims.

Another big plus: "You can use it with any style of eating because it's not about what you consume; it's about how you eat," tells Susan Albers, Psy. D., EatQ's best-selling New York Times writer, and a thoughtful food specialist. That implies, whether you're paleo, vegan, or gluten-free, you can know how to exercise mindful eating not only to assist you to adhere to your favorite style of food but also to appreciate more than you would otherwise understand.

Finally, mindful eating is all about enhancing your connection with food. "It helps crack a person's food grip," suggests Amanda Kozimor-Perrin R.D.N., a dietitian centered in LA. "It begins to, assist in eliminating the concept that food is' excellent' or' bad' and hopefully prevents ongoing yo-yo consumption." Mindfulness and awareness can also assist decrease stress, generally by adopting current methods such as meditation, practice, and baths that substitute emotional eating.

How to Know If Mindful Eating Is Right for You

Don't know if this is the correct working mode for you? Spoiler Alert: Mindful eating is for everybody.

"Everyone is a contestant for a mindful living style," states Amy Goldsmith, R.D.N., a dietitian living in Frederick, MD. "Most people lose their hunger and satiety intuitiveness around the era of 5 or when they join the education scheme, merely because they move from eating when they need the energy to eat when they have a time limit." Think about it: you were likely told f. This makes logistical sense when you're a kid, but one of the most excellent stuff about being an adult is that you can do what you want when you want, right?! That can and should include eating. Now, that doesn't imply that exercising mindfulness and eating will be unaffected. "It's not going to stick if you're not prepared to create adjustments to your lifestyle," tells Kozimor-Perrin. "All of us, when we introduce fresh conduct or try to modify our present ones, need to be prepared for that shift so that when it's difficult, we move through." Just like with any diet shift, you'll need to create a dedication to see the adjustments you're searching for regardless of whether they're mental or physical.

How to Eat Mindfully

One of the greatest things about teaching how to be a thoughtful eater is that you can describe what it implies for you as a person rather than conform to the norms set. "Think instruments, not regulations." But the abstract nature of mindful eating can also render it harder to enforce than a more rigid rules-based eating style. This can sometimes be discouraging to individuals used to know precisely how to consume. Luckily, there are a lot of policies you can attempt to get started on your own.

Be an observer, man. "People are surprised when I give them Step One: Don't do anything distinct," Albers suggests. "Don't spend a solid week observing your eating habits. That means just noticing without adding any comments (i.e.,' how could I be so stupid?') Judgment shuts down awareness on a dime." You'll probably be surprised at how many eating habits you've had that you didn't even know were habits, she claims. "For instance, one of my customers said that she held her eyes open for a week. She discovered that she ate thoughtlessly only when she was in front of the displays. She became very conscious of this practice. This knowledge was life-changing for her." Try the sit-down, slow down, savor, simplify, and smile. These are the fundamental principles of mindful eating, and with some exercise, they're going to become second nature before you realize it. "Sit down when you're eating," Albers says. "It looks simple, but you'll be amazed how often you eat while sitting. We consume 5% more when sitting. Slowing down helps break down the meals and provides you time to contemplate each piece." If this is hard for you, she advises eating with your nondominant side, which will force you to take shorter bites. Savoring implies using all your senses when you're eating. "Don't just throw the meat; determine if you like it." Simplify involves developing a mind-full eating atmosphere. When you've finished eating, placed your meals out of sight. "This decreases the temptation to grab meals unconsciously just because it's there." Finally, "smile between bites," Albers suggests. It might sound strange, but it'll offer you a time to determine if you're delighted.

Take a step back from the displays. Make it a ditch screen policy when you're dining. "Put off your mobile, sit down and slow down," Taitz suggests. "To be careful, you need to be active, and you can't be present when you're clicking or hurrying." Schedule time for your meals and snacks. Comparably, attempt to maintain functioning and eating distinct. "We function in a community that operates through breakfast and dinner, has lengthy journeys to work, or skips snack and dinner breaks," Goldsmith claims. "Add breaks to your timetable and let yourself be honored." You can spare 15 minutes, correct?

Try this raisin experiment. "I invite everyone I meet to do a raisin experiment," states Kozimor-Perrin. Inherently, the raisin experiment guides you through the basics of mindful eating by knowing every small aspect of a little raisin. "It looks very awkward at first, but it enables you to understand all the elements that are lacking to be present during dinner, leading to a light bulb in your brain. It enables you to see how you should take your time with food and how to start to understand your connection with each food you eat." Make sure you have access to meals that you like to eat. While mindful eating doesn't dictate what kind of meals you should consume, you'll likely feel best if you concentrate on reasonable, right ingredients most of the time even though there's plenty of space for indulgences. "Ensure that you have grocery stores to create or carry food," Goldsmith claims. "If that's not feasible, choose restaurants that provide you with the appropriate food you need, such as a blend of protein, grain, fruit, vegetables, and milk."

CHAPTER 5
UNDERSTANDING EMOTIONAL EATING

Eating for enjoyment or eating to decrease daily stress is two ends of the same coin, but our all-or-nothing minds split this indivisible coin into Emotional half eating is misunderstood and often unduly demonized. Emotional eating, that is, eating to feel beautiful, commonly referred to as "compulsive overeating is not an issue. It's mental over-eating and mindless emotional eating that can be both psychologically and physically unhealthful. Emotional eating operates as a coping strategy and a stress reliever when approached with mindfulness and moderation.

Emotional Eating Is Inevitable

Whether you consume or overeat, whether you drink thoughtfully or thoughtlessly, one thing is evident: individuals only consume what they like to consume. How a specific food taste is mostly emotional.

Let's face it: your body doesn't give a hoot, whether you eat something that tastes good or not, as long as the food isn't spoiled. Taste is a matter of mind, a matter of enjoyment. Bottom row: Everyone eats for entertainment, so it's natural to eat emotionally.

Emotional Eating Is Coping

Aside from emotional eating to feeling nice, some of us are also eating to deal with — that is, to decrease mental suffering. Eating for life or eating to reduce daily stress is two ends of the same coin, but our all-or-nothing minds split this indivisible coin in half. On the one side, we are urged to slow down and appreciate the meals that we consume. On the other hand, popular culture tells us never to destroy for mental purposes. If that feels like hypocrisy, that's it. At the same time, any pursuit of well-being is a decrease in trouble.

Why Emotional Eating Works

There are several excellent factors why emotional eating is as attractive as dealing.

Eating is verbal coping: from day one, feeding was the standard parenting option, and the pacifier was our first coping instrument. Eating to relieve oral stress, for instance, after quitting smoking, is a comfortable and relaxing option.

Feeding is caring: many cultures explicitly associate feeding with caring. Remember Grandma's home-baked chocolate cookies after a tough day at college?

Mealtime is time for assistance. Family meals are a family ritual and, at best, a time of togetherness, an opportunity for social relations and belonging and a means of emotional well-being.

Eating is being grounded. Consumption is a ritual, and as such, it is reassuring in its predictability. Waste is an entertaining, unmistakably physical exercise. As such, eating is an efficient truth check in a moment of uncertainty or confusion, conduct that causes and centers a busy or overworked mind.

Eating is so enjoyable. From a physiological point of view, the decision of consumption can be seen as an effort to immediately control the nervous system by turning on the portion of our wiring that is connected with relaxation and remainder.

Leveraging More Coping Per Calorie Given that we all consume socially at some stage or another, here are a few suggestions for creating your meals more thoughtful, efficient, ground-breaking, enjoyable and nutritionally beneficial: accept emotional eating as a valid coping option, not a coping failure.

When you eat to deal, first have an appetizer of relaxation. Take a couple of times to recognize your breath and smell your meals. Preload the fullness of the time.

Follow a regular ritual of eating, with a definite beginning and finishing points. Start breathing, concentrate on your meals throughout your dinner, and end up with a good dose of self-acceptance.

Use pattern-interruption methods (such as eating with a non-dominant side or using the incorrect utensils) to maintain your mind conscious of, guess, present, and concentrated during the emotional eating session.

If you want to binge or "veg out," go back to a sort of mindless "hand-to-mouth" trance, then find a harm-reduction approach: carefully choose what you're going to consume. Instead of "inhaling" a bag of M&Ms, fill in the carrot sticks. The argument that carrot sticks do not smell as lovely as M&Ms is meaningless here. Remember, this "hand-to-mouth" dance is not about flavor, after all, but about the relaxing exercise of self-feeding.

Know the convenience of your food. Mindful emotional eating is a self-care effort. So, if you're planning to attempt self-medication with meals, you might as well use the correct "medication." Allow yourself to have precisely the experience of enjoyment you're looking for. Or risk filling up on what you don't want to consume, and then feeling twice as unhappy.

Indulge in quality, not quantity. Mindful emotional eating is not about fulfilling your caloric quota or how much you're eating, but about how much you're enjoying this time of eating. So, when you buy your comfort food, pay the premium rate, get the top-quality food. This extra financial investment is probable to intrigue your tongue and assists you to slow down to realize this time of self-care.

Just eat when you consume to deal with it. The proposal of "eating when you're eating" is the cornerstone of any mindful eating understand how. It's particularly crucial when it comes to mindful emotional eating. When you sit down to eat to deal, switch off the TV, set the reading aside. Or risk losing out on the very time of self-care that you have so bravely permitted yourself to have. So, when you're eating to deal with it, then you have to sell. If meals are your therapist right now, then you have to sign up with yourself for this meeting.

CHAPTER 6
HOW TO EFFECTIVELY DEAL WITH EATING URGES AND BUILD SELF-CONFIDENCE

Researchers have a hard time deciding precisely what self-confidence is. Some claim that you merely believe in yourself, while others go into more detail about your expectations and assessments of yourself and your achievement.

For non-academic reasons, however, we have a reasonably strong concept of "our self-confidence in trusting our skills, skills, and opinions; the conviction that we can satisfy the requirements of a task." This concept operates reasonably well for the average person and is simple to comprehend. Being confident is trusting in our abilities and thinking that we can do what we set our minds to do.

As you can see from the notion, self-confidence is a necessary but not sufficient part of confidence. You must have at least some degree of self-confidence, but merely self-confidence does not necessarily ensure self-confidence.

In addition to characterizing your views about yourself, self-confidence is a characteristic that permeates your ideas, emotions, and behavior. Think about a confident individual you understand; now, believe about how comfortable you know that individual is. You can't get inside their heads to discover how they feel about themselves, so you base your decision on their self-confidence on their phrases and behavior.

To be genuinely self-confident is to exude trust in your words and deeds, about believing in yourself and feeling capable of doing so.

Three of the essential concepts that molded our understanding of self-confidence are William James ' self-esteem "formula," Bandura's Self-Efficacy Theory, and Deci and Ryan's Self-Determination Theory.

Thanks to William James, we've discovered that self-confidence is a significant predictor of achievement. His formula for self-esteem (an associated but mildly distinct structure than confidence) suggests that it is constructed on the basis of two elements: how we think and what we think about ourselves (our self-confidence / self-confidence) This idea was not a fresh one, but James was one of the first to write it down in detail. The concept stuck and affected the job of another significant idea in the field of self-confidence and self-esteem: Bandura's Theory of Self-Efficacy.

Bandura's theory states that self-efficacy is built on one's belief in the likelihood of future success; those who believe they have the ability to influence the events of their lives have a high degree of self-efficacy, while those who feel they are not in control and have little or no impact on what happens to them in the future have a low degree of self-efficacy.

Self-efficiency focuses on present views about the future; while self-confidence also concerns opinions about the future, there is a clear connection to the past; after all, our confidence is constructed on our previous experiences.

Deci and Ryan borrowed from Bandura's job to develop their concept of another self-construction: self-esteem. Self-Determination Theory argues that we are all born with an intrinsic desire to discover our work and thrive, and that self-esteem is the consequence of fundamental human requirements being met: Relatedness Competence Autonomy (Ryan & Deci, 2000) This concept broadens the limits of self-confidence/self-esteem literature by adding to the needs element; when our demands are encountered, according to their.

Based on these three theories and numerous other accounts, papers, and research by other scientists in the sector, we have been prepared to create a more consistent image of what self-confidence is. It's a sense of confidence and a sense of assurance of your skills and opportunities for potential achievement, and it's mostly based on your previous experience.

Self-confidence vs. Self-esteem So, although confidence and self-esteem have passed routes at many points and share some common characteristics, they are regarded to be two separate constructs.

Self-esteem is a relatively stable feature that does not alter much in individuals— unless they make a devoted attempt to enhance it. It can usually be described as our belief in our inherent value, value, and how worthy we are of love, happiness, achievement, and other excellent stuff in existence.

Self-confidence, on the other hand, does not take into account any belief in worthiness or overall value; instead, it focuses on the ability to succeed and the confidence in one's likelihood of success.

They are positively related, but it is easy to see where the line is drawn between them; self-esteem is about the success you feel you deserve, while self-confidence is about the progress you think you are capable of achieving.

Research on self-confidence Research on self-confidence has given us with useful ideas that relate to a broad spectrum of fields of existence. Check out the results in each of the seven themes mentioned below.

Use of Self-Confidence Issues Cognitive Behavioral Therapy (CBT) helps enhance self-confidence among other types of treatment. The objective is to alter dysfunctional habits of thinking and substitute them with functional, safe practices of thinking.

Four primary methods for self-confidence may be used in CBT: cognitive restructuring Systematic exposure Mindfulness training problem-solving the importance of confidence Not only does it merely feel pleasant to think in yourself, self-confidence and self-confidence also deliver other desirable advantages.

The research has shown that people with elevated self-confidence enjoy better general health because they are better at coping with stress and hard feelings.

More time for their relatives and colleagues, because they tend to set reasonable limits and abandon job in the office.

Better relationships due to good boundary-setting and capacity to concentrate and enhance functional interactions.

Concerning these advantages, Dr. TC North lists 12 positions from boosting self-confidence. Not all of them are backed up by a lot of studies, but they all seem like probable results of higher confidence: improved coping and flourishing under stress Improved capacity to impact and convince others More management and corporate presence Increased favorable attitude Improved sense of feeling appreciated (by yourself and probably others as well) Improved efficiency at job

You may also suffer from self-limiting views; these are attitudes that somehow restrict or constrain us, and prevent us from thinking, saying, or doing stuff we want to do and material that can assist us in developing.

These self-limiting views usually fit into one of the following categories: I do/don't—restricting opinions about how we describe ourselves.

I can't—limit our views in terms of self-image and self-efficacy.

I shouldn't —limit the belief that keeps us caught in self-judgment and even self-shame.

I am/am not—restricting the belief that is centered on what we are or are not (e.g., "I am smart" vs. "I am dumb").

Others are/will be restricting the belief that focuses on other individuals and what we think they are imagining.

If you discover yourself falling into any of these traps, you've come to the correct location! Keep reading, and you'll see some helpful advice, suggestions, drills, and workbooks that can help you build confidence.

Self-confidence and belief in sport As you might think, the study has shown that self-esteem and confidence are incredibly crucial in athletics. In reality, it is so critical that a meta-analysis of self-confidence and sports results has discovered an impact magnitude of.24 (Woodman & Hardy, 2003). These can be viewed (approximately) as stating that self-confidence accounts for about 24 percent of the output variability!

The meta-analysis was based on 48 distinct research and also discovered some other exciting findings: although cognitive performance anxiety was also substantially linked to performance, its effect size was much smaller than that of self-confidence.

Self-confidence and anxiety have a much more significant impact on men's results than on women's performance, although this may be a measure or a tiny sample size of females.

These results back up what trainers everywhere have been stating for centuries: some sort of "you have to trust in yourself to succeed." The function of self-confidence in relationships Belief in yourself performs a significant part in the fulfillment of both your own and that of your spouse.

The research by Erol and Orth explored the impact that self-esteem has on family performance and discovered that self-esteem is a vital predictor of the fulfillment of one's partnership, as well as the happiness of one's collaboration or spouse. This impact has been noted in five distinct research and across interactions of all duration between individuals of all sizes.

Those with a reasonable rate of self-esteem usually have a safe attachment style and appreciate higher fulfillment in their relationship, especially when they are in connection with another elevated self-esteem person.

The impact of self-confidence on friendships is so significant that it can even suggest modified methods of thinking about your spouse. A research of this subject discovered that those with poor self-esteem are less willing to incorporate favorable and adverse thoughts about their partner, and tend to fall victim to "all-or-nothing" or black and white thinking either their partner is great and their connection is incredible, or their partner is a burden and their relationship is terrible (Graham & Clark, 2006).

As you might imagine, self-confidence in management is very crucial. Some go as far as stating, "There is no management without trust.

Leadership needs healthy decision-making, courageous but measured risk-taking and engagement: three items that are usually lacking or lagged in those with reduced self-confidence.

As Dao states, self-confidence is also essential for staff to see themselves as rulers; nothing boosts workers ' faith in the organization and their contributions other than to see trust and comparable confidence in the management of the organization.

In reality, self-confidence was recognized as one of the defining features of rulers in relevant new management research (Mowday, 1979). Efficient management needs at least a minimum amount of self-confidence.

The benefits of self-confidence in the workplace Although confidence is essential to politicians, and it is also crucial to the rank and file.

A good feeling of self-confidence can lead in many advantages appropriate to the workforce, including more exceptional optimism Ability to conduct gatherings efficiently and confidently More efficient delegation A more excellent feeling of autonomy More frequent promotions and higher positions Higher pay and more regular wage increases (RIVS, n.d.).

CHAPTER 7
DEVELOP A LIFESTYLE OF HEALTHY EATING

1. Get the equilibrium.

Eat a diet of 45 percent carbs, 30 percent protein, and 35 percent good-for-your-fat olive oil, seafood or vegetables. "Eating too little fat causes you feel ashamed of yourself," Forberg suggests. "Sprinkle the almonds on your salad, add the Parmesan cheese on your whole-wheat pasta, or wrap the avocado on your sandwich. Fat is a flavor provider that enables other items to feel stronger."

2. Avoid doing anything artificial.

Stick with authentic ingredients such as vegetables, fruit, nuts, lean meat, low-fat milk and whole-grain pasta, rice, and bread. "The concept is to get the largest calorie buck nutrient bang. Processed foods involve a bunch of junk. Real products are antioxidant-rich and fiber-filled."

3. Pile on the green stuff, man.

"The majority of your diet should be vegetables such as tomatoes, mushrooms, zucchini, spinach, and other greens," Forberg suggests. Vegetables are caught in the fiber and the water that fills you. "You're going to be amazed by how much you can consume if you pursue this plan."

4. Keep a diary of meals.

"People who write down what they consume after every dinner lose half the weight of those who do not."

5. Set a good limit.

"At the display, we suggest that females eat between 1,200 and 1,500 calories a day and that males eat between 1,600 and 2,400 calories a day, based on their age," suggests Forberg. "If you're tired, consume a little more. It's about changing your lifestyle and doing something viable.

Knowing What Your Body Needs.

It was an extraordinary achievement that gave birth to a batch of crazy scientist-like self-experiments to find out an available nutritional link to my skin disease. What I discovered blew my mind: mushrooms, eggplants, milk, and peanut butter all caused my eczema. As quickly as I eliminated them, my skin calmed down, and my itchiness gradually vanished, and, strangely enough, my sleep also began to improve. My body was screaming at me all this moment, but I refused to hear.

The advice to "listen to your body" sounds noble, but in practice, it's as useful as telling someone, "Don't believe of a tap-dancing bear in a top hat." A lot of that has to do with contemporary distractions. "In the 21st century, we're encircled by items that are stronger than our body's signals or interrupt those evolutionary feedback loops," I was advised by Dr. Krista Scott-Dixon, Ph.D., Director of Education at Precision Nutrition. Now you don't need eczema to understand that your body might be dissatisfied with what you're doing. Take sleepiness, for instance. We're united by artificial lights and technology that interrupt our natural patterns; if we feel a little tired, it's a jumbo-sized rescue coffee! Pretty quickly this becomes the norm, so even if the body is whining a little, we're going through it.

So, what are some of these bodily signals, precisely? Dr. Scott-Dixon says your energy levels are significant, saying, "It's not just about complete concentrations, it's about swings, too. Do you have ups and downs, or is your energy pretty coherent? Do you feel' wired and weary' like that? "Other active indices include recurrent pain, how often you get ill, mood, sex drive, digestion, and weight gain.

Sometimes, however, these signals may be "ordinary" if you try something fresh. "We often don't understand what's common or not normal," says Dr. Brian Wansink, writer of "Slim By Design." He states that if you modify the kinds of food you consume, it might be okay to get a headache, feel a little more exhausted, or have more cravings for a few days as your body adjusts. But if you get dizzy when you stand up, for instance, that's the kind of symptom that you need to watch out for.

Paying attention to your body is one thing, but learning to receive feedback and transform it into something actionable is another thing. It took me a little sleuthing to find out my hints (like my eczema), so it might be useful to maintain a journal. Record what you ate, when you fell asleep and woke up, your mood and energy levels, etc. "Sometimes, patterns pop out right away, like' every moment I consume food X, I can't stop eating' or' every time I eat food Y, I get a headache.' Your body's signals can be hard to decipher, but just like anything else, it's a skill you can get good at improving your standard of life.

If you want to understand how to put an end to emotional eating, thanks. It requires an influential individual to acknowledge that they might be doing this.

Let's start by identifying what emotional eating truly is. It's eating when a particular incidence (or set of frequencies) occurs that generates an "elevated" or "low" sensation for someone. For instance, after a miserable day at the job, someone might find consolation in nutrition, a battle with a loved one. Or something tiny, like getting to park in a bunch of traffic before a job.

Conversely, you could consume mentally when beautiful things are going on. People often get more weight when they're in interactions because they're so pleased and convenient.

It's essential to recognize that sometimes individuals get invitations to consume meat for purposes that have little to do with being starving, but more to cater to our wishes. We understand the desire to drink, and we believe that the only remedy for these temptations is to consume fattening products (and in actuality, more good activities can be achieved).

Emotional eating only contributes to downward spirals because it makes the issue worse because it provides to emotions of guilt, weight carrying, and, generally, poor nutrition for the body.

It's a beautiful thing that you're searching for data on how to stop eating emotionally.

Some things you can do right away are to find out why you're eating mentally and what kind of occurrences make you do this. You can also find out when you're starving, and not when you want to consume mentally.

Finally, we posed two problems concerning emotional eating. We challenged the legitimacy of self-reported psychological eating questionnaires and debated alternative interpretations of these interventions. The hypothesis that emotional eating questionnaires are appropriate indicators of eating conduct in reaction to adverse feelings is no longer tenable, as demonstrated by the number of research showing no enhanced consumption of meat in adverse moods by self-reported mental eaters. Together with the mild to robust correlations between emotional eating and other signs of overeating or eating concern, these findings indicate that the notion of emotional eating is more complicated than is often assumed to be. Although the exact nature of emotional eating remains elusive, it is clear that current questionnaires cannot be used to evaluate this behavior, and there will probably be more emotional eating than raising the consumption of meat, especially when in a negative mood. Researchers interpreting findings based on self-reported psychological eating interventions, whether in their information or the outcomes of others, should be cautious and critical when doing so.

65

www.ingramcontent.com/pod-product-compliance
Lightning Source LLC
La Vergne TN
LVHW090018180726
843489LV00008B/2848